All that glitters

The parable of the unforgiving servant

Chris Hudson

Acknowledgments

We would like to thank Wylva Davies and Val Bulman for their help. We would also like to express our gratitude to the following schools for trialling the material.

St Mark's C of E, Worsley, Manchester
Parkview Primary, Oakwood, Derby
St Andrew's Primary, Salisbury
Holy Trinity Primary, Bradley Stoke, Bristol

The Stapleford Centre is an interdenominational centre which aims to produce materials, and offer in-service courses, to resource the teaching of Christianity in schools. Full details of courses and publications are available from:

The Stapleford Centre
The Old Lace Mill
Frederick Road
Stapleford
Nottingham
NG9 8FN
Tel: 0115 939 6270
Fax: 0115 939 2076
E-mail: admin@stapleford-centre.org
Website: www.stapleford-centre.org

Text copyright © Chris Hudson 2001
Illustrations copyright © Jane Taylor 2001

The author asserts the moral right
to be identified as the author of this work

Published by
The Bible Reading Fellowship
First Floor, Elsfield Hall
15–17 Elsfield Way, Oxford OX2 8FG
ISBN 1 84101 207 6
First published 2001
10 9 8 7 6 5 4 3 2 1 0
All rights reserved

Acknowledgments
Unless otherwise stated, scripture quotations are taken from the Good News Bible published by
The Bible Societies/HarperCollins Publishers Ltd UK © American Bible Society 1966, 1971, 1976,
1992, used with permission

A catalogue record for this book is available from the British Library

Printed and bound in Malta

Contents

How to use this book 4

All that glitters 5

Activity bank 23–24

Literacy worksheets 25–28

RE teacher's page 29

RE worksheets 30–32

How to use this book

This book provides the following:
- ★ Masters for a Big Book
- ★ Activities for literacy work (word, sentence and text level)
- ★ RE follow-up ideas
- ★ RE activity sheets/stimulus material
- ★ Differentiated RE activities
- ★ Ideas for reflection/learning from religion

Parables

Parables are stories with a spiritual/moral meaning. They are an example of non-literal language, along with metaphors and similes.

RE and literacy work

As well as the Big Book masters, this book contains a bank of activities at word, sentence and text level; literacy activity sheets; RE follow-up and RE activity sheets. There is some information for teachers on some of the activity sheets; this can be removed using office 'white-out' before copying. The material in this book can be used in RE and literacy time but the focus will be different in literacy and RE. Literacy teaching should not replace RE; neither should RE replace literacy teaching.

The Big Book

The story can be used in RE or literacy time. The masters for the Big Book can be used in a number of ways:
- ★ Photocopied on to acetates
- ★ Enlarged and photocopied to create a Big Book
- ★ Photocopied to create small pupil books

The pictures can be coloured either by hand or by scanning into the computer and using a paint programme on parts of the drawings. (Some software can do this.)

Suggested activities

- ★ Use items in the text to tell the story.
- ★ Pupils can mime or role-play situations in the story.
- ★ Ask questions about possible consequences of actions and what might happen next.
- ★ Bring out any moral issues for discussion: 'Do you think the Caliph was right to…?'
- ★ Ask pupils to read sections with appropriate expression.
- ★ Ask their opinion about what is happening in the story.
- ★ Relate the issues in the story to pupils' experiences.

QCA links (England)

Parables link to the following units in the QCA RE schemes: 1D, 2B, 3C, 3D, 5C, 5D, 6C and 6F.

Handling biblical material

Pupils should be told where the story comes from and why it is important to Christians. Christian material should be introduced: 'Today we are looking at a story from the Bible (or based on a story from the Bible) which is important to Christians.' This allows pupils to identify with the story or to study it from another perspective.

All that glitters

There is a saying: all that glitters is not gold. Since ancient times, gold has been a precious metal. It doesn't rust or tarnish. A goldsmith uses it to create fine, beautiful jewellery. Gold has always been expensive because it is so rare. It is usually found underground in rock that has to be mined. The rock is crushed and heated until the gold pours out. It is dangerous work to separate the metal from the rock.

In the past, people called alchemists have tried to create gold out of other materials. History tells us that none of them succeeded; but there was, once, an alchemist who nearly discovered something that was even more precious.

There was a loud knocking on the front door – it sounded like someone in a hurry. Josiah put down the pot he was carrying and went to answer it. He opened the door to see a thin man dressed in simple but well-made robes – an official from the palace – accompanied by two burly palace guards who looked as if they were enjoying the outing.

The official spoke. 'His Wonderfulness the Caliph has sent for you. It's about some money that you owe him.'

Josiah was terrified. 'Already? But it hasn't worked yet! There's nothing to show him!'

'His Wonderfulness has sent letters demanding an explanation. Haven't you read them?'

Josiah looked nervous. 'Yes, but I'm so close! You don't know how close! I'm nearly there! Look, come in and I'll show you!'

He beckoned the official and the guards inside, led them along a passage to another room, pushed a thick curtain to one side – and, immediately, they started coughing. The ceiling was covered in darkening clouds of thick smoke. In a corner, something was burning over a fire, and the fumes were getting thicker.

'Give me some air!' the official spluttered. Josiah hurried to open a door that led out to the back yard. The official staggered outside, closely followed by the guards and another cloud of black smoke. Once in the yard, they were bent over, coughing, wheezing, straining to breathe in lungful after lungful of good, clean, morning air – and then one of the guards was sick.

'What were you trying to do – poison us?' gasped the official. 'The Caliph will hear about this!'

'No!' cried Josiah. 'You came in the middle of the experiment! There wasn't enough sulphur! I didn't have enough ingredients! That's where the money's gone, but I'm nearly there! Look!'

He dashed back into the smoke-filled room and returned with the vessel that had been heating up over the fire. He laid it on the ground, then fetched and poured into it a jug of cold water. The hot vessel hissed and crackled, producing more dense clouds – only now it was steam. The others gazed on the scene, now fascinated. Who was this fool?

Then there was a cry of delight from the alchemist as he stared into the vessel.

'Look! I've done it! I've really done it! I've produced gold!' He pointed, shouting it out to the world. 'Do you hear it? Gold! Yes!'

The others looked at each other, wondering what to do next. This changed everything.

Even the Caliph was surprised, and that took some doing — especially after lunch.

'So, my alchemist has finally succeeded?'

'Yes, Your Wonderfulness!' The official and the guards had brought Josiah and his vessel to the palace.

'Show me your gold then, Alchemist.' Josiah stepped forward towards the royal throne to show both the vessel and the gleaming residue that lay at the bottom. 'And that, presumably, is gold?' There was the hint of a doubt in the Caliph's voice.

'I have to test it, but yes, I think so, your Wonderfulness.'

'You have created this gold out of nothing?'

'Not quite nothing, your Wonderfulness. I had to send to many other lands for the ingredients, and look in many libraries to find the way to do it. This has indeed cost a great deal.'

'According to my Chancellor, it has cost ten thousand talents. Alchemist, your research has cost me a great deal of gold, more than you said at the beginning.'

He stared into the vessel again. 'Have you made any more?' The alchemist looked shamefaced, and the Caliph frowned. 'I take it, this means that you haven't. So then, you have taken ten thousand talents from my royal purse to produce a tiny gleam of metal that, even if it was gold, would only be worth one talent, if that. Most alchemists try to turn simple metals into gold, but my royal alchemist has gone one further – he has turned gold into rubbish!'

The Caliph rose to his feet, glaring. 'You have wasted my money, and made me a fool for trusting you! Well then – you can do what everyone else has to do. Pay it back!'

The alchemist was horrified. 'Pay back ten thousand talents? But I'm only a humble servant, Your Wonderfulness! The money's gone, you know that! How could I pay off that sort of debt?'

'You managed to spend it quickly enough! Perhaps this will concentrate your mind a little so that you can produce a little more gold from somewhere!'

The alchemist's mind raced. He tried to think of places where he had some money. About two talents of the Caliph's money was hidden under the floor of his laboratory – but a lot had been spent on ingredients for experiments that hadn't worked. He'd even lent some money to a few other people, but getting them to pay it back still wouldn't raise enough to pay back the Caliph. This was all going badly wrong.

Josiah realized that he was running out of ideas.
'But there isn't any more money anywhere!
All I have is my laboratory, my house,
my wife and my children!'
The Caliph was furious.
'Let them be sold as slaves then!'

Slaves? The alchemist thought of his beloved wife, who always nagged him when he borrowed a kitchen bowl and didn't return it, and then forgave him with a kiss. He thought of his three children. He imagined them all being taken, auctioned and sold in the market place to the highest bidder, like so many cattle. Then he thought of his laboratory, with all his tools and instruments and ingredients being taken and scattered. This was awful! He fell to his knees.

'Please, Your Wonderfulness! I'm only a simple alchemist! I was only serving you! Yes, the money's gone, and no, I can't say for sure if there is gold in that vessel, but... I can't pay it back! I never will because I can't! Please – tearing my family and household apart won't give you back your ten thousand talents! I'm sorry! I was too ambitious! I should have discussed it more with you at an earlier date! I'm sorry, I really am!' There were others in the throne room, but it fell strangely silent as the royal alchemist began to cry.

Then there was a cough, a clearing of the throat from the direction of the throne. 'Enough of this. Get out.' What was that? The alchemist stared up at the Caliph, who was speaking to him. 'You heard. Out! It's my fault for trusting an alchemist and not keeping an eye on him. I've brought this on myself, even though it's you who have wasted everything.'

'Pardon, Your Wonderfulness?'

'I'm forgiving you, man! Now get out of here before I change my mind! Don't come back. Take this stinking bowl with you.' He thrust it at the alchemist, who took it, rose from his knees, bowed, and left the room – quickly.

Josiah couldn't believe his luck! It had worked! He'd been forgiven the whole debt, and he still had some of it hidden away! He couldn't believe it. Perhaps the Caliph was having a good day, or he'd fallen in love, or something.

Josiah strolled out into the afternoon sunshine, blinking at its brightness, amazed that he still had his freedom. Now was the time to make plans. Perhaps he could go and work for another ruler. There was bound to be someone else who would pay him to make gold. He saw a pile of rubbish by the roadside and, smiling, threw the vessel on the top. Of course there hadn't been any gold in there. He'd known that all along.

He hurried home, not wanting to waste any more time. His family could be out of the house and on the road in a week, and in a month he could be working for someone else in another country.

The rich will always pay up if there's a chance of becoming even richer! He smiled. What a day! This was turning out even better than he'd dreamed. Once home, he opened an account book to find out who owed him money, drew up a list of names, and then went out visiting, calling in all the debts.

It all went smoothly. A lot of people seemed to think he still worked for the Caliph, which made them pay up more quickly – a few gold coins here, and some silver there. He ticked the names off the list as his money bag filled up.

Then he came to the last name: Reuben, a servant who worked in the palace kitchens, still owed him five silver pieces. It wasn't a lot, but Josiah decided it was worth the fuss. He found the right house, knocked on the door, and explained himself.

'But I can't pay now!' Reuben said.

'Why not?'

'I just don't have it. Can't it wait until 'the end of the month, when I get paid?'

'No! I need it now!'

'I haven't got it now! You'll have to wait!' The door slammed shut, and Josiah stormed off down the dark street. He knew how to sort out Reuben.

A few days later, the alchemist was back in the throne room, standing between two guards, the same ones who'd brought him in last time. They looked rather pleased with themselves.

'Let me see...' mused the Caliph, reading the note in his hand. 'Last week I said I didn't want to see you again. Do you remember that?' The alchemist nodded. 'Good,' continued the Caliph. 'I remember cancelling your debt of ten thousand talents. Do you remember that too?'

The alchemist nodded again, nervously. 'Good. Since then, my cook has been to see me. One of the people who work in the palace kitchens has apparently been put in jail because he owes you some money. Is that correct?' Josiah nodded, nervously licking his lips.

'Now tell me, Alchemist — exactly how much did he owe you?' There was a silence. 'How much, Alchemist?'

'Five pieces of silver.'

'I see. Five pieces of silver. Just remind me again, how much were you forgiven?'

'Ten thousand talents.'

'And you put a person in jail for five miserable pieces of silver — the cost of a good meal. Well, it's clear that you believe in fairness, don't you?'

The alchemist nodded.

'Well then, I shall be fair. You owed me ten thousand talents. I am now demanding it from you again, since you obviously don't believe in the quality of mercy and forgiveness. You can go to jail and work out a way to pay your debt, since you obviously think that all debts should be paid. Is that clear? Alchemist, is that clear enough for you?'

It was. The alchemist was taken away — and, like the Caliph's gold, he was never seen again.

Activity Bank

Word level

Year 5

TERM 1

(W7) Collect and classify examples of alternatives for 'said' in the text. Extension: discuss what these alternatives contribute to character development.

(W7) Find/brainstorm synonyms for 'coughing' and 'dashed' on pages 8 and 9.

TERM 2

(W3) Research words with the prefix 'gold-'. Study the use/origins of the suffix '-smith'. Extension: collect/invent other words using that suffix, and use them in sentences.

(W5) Investigate words with common letter strings: '-ough' on page 16.

TERM 3

(W12, W13) Brainstorm word meanings (Worksheet B), then research definitions.

(W6) Transform words by changing their tense. Find examples/variations on page 6.

Year 6

TERM 1

(W3, W10) Find related words to: 'create', 'terrified', 'explanation', 'succeeded', 'official'.

(W4) Revise unstressed vowels in polysyllabic words on page 5: 'jewellery', 'separate'.

TERM 2

(W3) Invent fantasy (adjectival) terms of respect in the vein of 'Your Wonderfulness'.

TERM 3

(W4) Study the use of the word 'lungful'. Brainstorm/list similar '-ful' words. Extension: how are they distinct from '-full' words? Is there a pattern or rule?

(W3) Research the meanings of unfamiliar words in the text (Worksheet B).

Sentence level

Year 5

TERM 1

(S5) Re-express a short passage of direct speech as reported speech to show differences.

TERM 2

(S8) Find examples of sentences with additional clauses that contribute further ideas. Extension: write alternative versions of these sentences, with new clauses.

TERM 3

(S7) Collect/sort the connectives used. For headings, see Worksheet C.

Year 6

TERM 1

(S1) Study the page 7 paragraph beginning 'He beckoned…', analysing sentences to see what would happen to the meaning if clauses were placed in a different order.

(S4, S5) Study use/effect of connectives (Worksheet C: for extension, omit word lists).

TERM 2

(S3) Study use of capitals, apart from starting sentences. List different types of proper noun.

(S4) Contract complex sentences in text by removing detail, converting into simple sentences, or finding key words to sum up key points.

TERM 3

(S1) Explanatory texts/narratives. Compare/contrast the opening paragraphs of pages 5 and 6.

(S1) Find and list phrases/sentences that convey the passing of time.

(S1) List different types of sentences used in the story under the following headings: statement, order, question, exclamation. Alternatively, highlight sections of the text.

▶

Text level

Year 5

TERM 1

Class: (T1) Study the story introduction. What mood and style does it establish?

Group: (T14) Key narrative features: beginning/ development/end. Summarize main events as short sentences. Identify main paragraph/key phrases/ sentences (Worksheet D).

Plenary: Share opinions on the main paragraph/key phrase/sentence in the story.

TERM 2

Class: (T2) Compare story/original parable (Worksheet A). Has the original meaning survived?

Group: (T8) Formal/informal narrative: tell the story from a guard's viewpoint (Worksheet D).

Plenary: Share some 'reports', and discuss what has been added to the narrative.

TERM 3

Class: (T14) Evaluate the layout/language of the back/front of the book for clues to contents.

Group: (T14) Write a story synopsis and an advertiser's blurb for the back of a video box cover.

Plenary: Share the writing, and compare with real-life examples of video covers.

Year 6

TERM 1

Class: (T5) Study the development of the alchemist's character. Which passage is most revealing?

Group: (T9) Turn a passage with dialogue into a short script, with stage directions.

(T1) Create a similar story based on this parable, but set in the present day.

Plenary: Perform some of the scripts, or share stories.

TERM 2

Class: (T1) Discuss narrative structure, especially over how the passage of time is conveyed.

Group: (T1) Create a story map/feelings graph to convey the main points of the narrative and the emotional career of the alchemist (Worksheet D).

(T1) Summarize the whole story in exactly fifty words.

(T1) This story has 18 pages. If the publisher wanted to cut about two pages, where would be the best places? How would this affect the story?

Plenary: Share and discuss some of the maps and graphs/summaries.

TERM 3

Class: (T12) Compare story/original parable (Worksheet A). Has the meaning been kept?

Group: (T22) Write a formal exchange of letters between the Caliph and the alchemist.

(T17, T18) Research alchemy as a topic, especially for connections with modern science.

Plenary: Feed back some of the letters and research.

Literacy Worksheet A

The parable of the unforgiving servant

There was once a king who was checking his accounts to find out who owed him money – and he found that one of his own servants actually owed him thousands of pounds! The servant was brought in, but couldn't pay, so the king ordered him to be sold as a slave, along with his family and possessions, to raise the cash. The servant fell to his knees. 'Please! Be patient with me! Give me more time, and I'll pay it all!' He looked so sad that the king went one step further, and actually forgave him the whole debt, and then let him go.

Then the man went outside, and chanced to meet another servant, who owed him a few pounds. He grabbed this man by the neck and started choking him in rage. 'Pay up what you owe me!' he shouted. This other man was terrified. 'I can't! Please, give me more time, and I'll pay it all!' The servant refused – and had this man thrown into jail until he could pay.

The other servants saw this happening, and were very upset – so much so, they went to tell the king, who called his servant back. 'What kind of person are you?' he demanded. 'I showed you mercy. I forgave you the whole amount that you owed, simply because you asked. Why couldn't you do the same for someone who owed you so much less?' This time, the king sent the man to jail to be punished until he paid back the whole amount that he owed.

BASED ON MATTHEW 18:23–34

Activity 1
Compare this story with 'All that glitters'. List what has been added in terms of **setting**, **characters**, **plot** and **events**. Has the original meaning of the parable been kept?

Activity 2
In a Bible, look up Matthew 18:21–35. What was the question that caused Jesus to tell this story? The answer to the question was a parable. Summarize the 'answer' in one sentence.

Literacy Worksheet B

This is a glossary of words used in the story 'All that glitters', with their definitions.

Activity 1

With a partner, play 'Definitions', where one player has the sheet and reads out the definition, while the other (with no sheet) has to guess which word goes with it.

Activity 2

Cut up the words and definitions, shuffle them and then turn them face down to play a version of 'Pairs' in which you have to match the word with its correct definition. Which of these words best sums up the meaning of the story? Give a reason for your answer.

Tarnish	When a metal loses its natural colour and gloss
Ancient	Very old – usually when talking about the past
Goldsmith	A person whose craft it is to make special objects out of gold
Alchemist	In the past, someone who tried to make precious metals out of other materials
Sulphur	A chemical that burns with a strong smell
Vessel	A container
Slave	A servant who is owned. A slave is the personal property of his or her owner
Auctioned	Sold in a marketplace to the person who 'bids' (offers) the highest price
Debt	Something you owe to someone else
Mercy	Showing kindness to someone who doesn't deserve it
Forgiveness	Letting go of hatred towards someone who has wronged you

Literacy Worksheet C

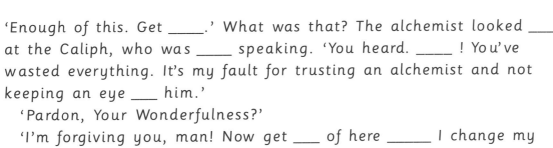

1. Connectives and conjunctions are words and phrases that give a text cohesion. From the box at the bottom, choose words to fill the gaps in the text, to help the passage below make sense. Afterwards, sum up the meaning of the passage in one sentence.

2. With a partner, generate some interesting connective phrases that would fill some of the gaps left by single words and tell us more about what is going on. This is easier in some places than others!

'Enough of this. Get ____.' What was that? The alchemist looked ___ at the Caliph, who was ____ speaking. 'You heard. ____ ! You've wasted everything. It's my fault for trusting an alchemist and not keeping an eye ___ him.'
  'Pardon, Your Wonderfulness?'
  'I'm forgiving you, man! Now get ___ of here ____ I change my mind! Don't come back. Take this stinking bowl ____ you.' He thrust it __ the alchemist, who took it, rose ____ his knees, bowed, and left the room – quickly.
  Josiah couldn't believe his luck! It had worked! He couldn't believe it. Perhaps the Caliph was having a good day, or he'd fallen __ love, or something. The alchemist strolled ____ ____ the afternoon sunshine, blinking at its brightness, amazed that he still had his freedom. ____ was the time to make plans. Perhaps he could go and work for _____ ruler. There was bound to be someone else who would pay him to try to make gold. He saw a pile of rubbish ___ the roadside and, smiling, threw the vessel ___ the top. Of course there hadn't been any gold __ there. He'd known that all along.

Connective collection
Location/position: at, by, from, in, in, into, on, on, out, out, out, out, up, with
Number/order: another
Time: before, now, now

27

Literacy Worksheet D

Activity 1

The story 'All that glitters' moves between several places, with most of the action taking place on one day. Create an imaginary map showing the position and order of the main events.

Activity 2

Josiah's feelings seem to change a lot during the course of the story. Create a 'feelings' line graph to show the 'highs' and 'lows' of his feelings as the story moves along. Your graph will need to have little labels that explain both the 'highs' and the 'lows', and the changes in between.

Activity 3

Each paragraph in this narrative has a part to play in telling the whole story. Select one large paragraph in the text and find out how it 'works' by listing the main events in it, and then summing up the paragraph's main theme in a few words.

Activity 4

The two palace guards would probably have had to keep a notebook that recorded everything that happened during their day. Write some entries for the days covered by this story. You will need to use your imagination to create some events and descriptions not covered by the story – for example, the arrest of Reuben.

Remember to keep this in formal language. It should be a record of what people said and did, but taken from the point of view of the guards. The dates and times are up to you – but, remember, they didn't tell the time as we do, or use the same calendar as us, so you can be creative!

'Date' – hmm... is it the Year of The camel, – or The Pickled Herring?

RE Teacher's Page

The story 'All that glitters' is based on the parable of the unforgiving servant (Matthew 18:21–35).

Story framework

(For use with 'All that glitters'.) Jesus liked to teach using stories called parables. This is a version of one of them. It was a response to a question by Peter about how many times he should forgive.

Background material

The Lord's Prayer includes a line asking God to 'forgive us our trespasses (or sins, or debts), as we forgive those who trespass against us'. The parable of the unforgiving servant explains the same link between God's forgiveness and human forgiveness – that you can't have one without the other.

The original parable mentions the servant as owing 'ten thousand talents' – in our understanding, that would be like owing millions of pounds. The magnitude of this debt underlines the ingratitude shown when the man accuses a fellow servant over the matter of a few silver pieces. The words 'debt' and 'sin' can be identical in Greek, the language of the New Testament.

Jesus was saying that God forgives people much more than they are ever called on to forgive others – so they should do it, anyway. Many people find this teaching difficult, either because they do not see themselves in need of God's forgiveness or because they cannot bring themselves to forgive the harm done to them. For Christians, forgiveness of others is a response to the forgiveness they feel they have received from God.

Forgiveness is about struggling to value the person despite their imperfections, and not allowing ourselves to be consumed by their crime. Without forgiveness, we condemn ourselves to living with hatred – and their crime lives on inside us. Forgiveness does not deny justice. It goes beyond justice to mercy. It is more than a person deserves.

Conversation starters

★ Do you think that the Caliph was fair? Why?
★ The alchemist seemed to be sorry when he was first taken to the palace. Was this real? How can you tell if someone is really sorry?
★ Why do you think the alchemist made such a fuss over a small amount of money when he had been forgiven so much?

Religious Education

RE activities

Worksheet E can be used either as a stimulus for discussion purposes or in its own right.

BASIC

Hear the original story as below, discuss the questions, and then sum up the message of the story in ten words or less.

STANDARD

Read the original Bible story of the unforgiving servant told by Jesus in Matthew 18:21–35, or use Worksheet A. Think and write about why the king was so angry at the end of the story. Write a short piece entitled 'What forgiveness means to me' that explains what you think forgiveness is, and how you think it applies to real life.

EXTENSION

Think of situations that you know of that could be helped if people were prepared to show more forgiveness to each other. Create a display using cuttings from national newspapers and magazines to illustrate this. (Choose suitable newspapers.)

Reflection/Learning from religion

Ask pupils to hold something in their fist – a rubber band would be suitable. Now ask them to let it go and watch it drop on the desk. Forgiveness is a letting go of hatred. Ask them to think about what they have learned about forgiveness from the story.

Teacher's note

The interview on pages 31–32 is intended to provoke discussion. Be aware that some of its content may be alarming for sensitive pupils.

Note: Please stress that forgiveness does not mean that a person escapes justice or that their crime is excused. It is about letting go of bitterness.

Activity 1

Read and discuss these statements about forgiveness, then think about how much you agree or disagree with each one, and mark this with a cross on the horizontal axis underneath.

Forgiveness is easy.

Agree _____ Disagree

You can't forgive someone who isn't sorry.

Agree _____ Disagree

Forgiveness is a way of controlling your anger.

Agree _____ Disagree

Forgiveness is about forgetting.

Agree _____ Disagree

You can forgive on behalf of someone else.

Agree _____ Disagree

Forgiveness helps you to leave your anger behind.

Agree _____ Disagree

It is wrong ever to let yourself get angry.

Agree _____ Disagree

Activity 2

★ Either: write about a time when you had to forgive somebody – or a time when you had to be forgiven.
★ Or: write about a situation in the news where forgiveness is needed.

What does it mean to forgive?

'Forgiveness' is a word that lots of people use, but they sometimes disagree about what it means. Michael Saward was a vicar who became famous in 1986 when he said he forgave the men who had broken into his house, attacking and seriously injuring him and the two other people who were in the building at the same time. (The men were later caught by the police, sentenced in court and sent to prison.) This 'exclusive' interview took place in March 2000.

Interviewer: Michael, what happened to you on 6 March in 1986?

Michael: Well, I was sitting in my study in Ealing Vicarage, where I was the vicar at the time, when the front doorbell rang. I went there, and I opened the door, and there was a man with a knife about an inch from my stomach. He had a balaclava on, with two other men who also had balaclavas on, and they came in screaming and shouting, wanting money which I hadn't got. They made me lie down on the floor. I didn't know that, in the meantime, they had found an old cricket bat of mine, and the next thing I knew, I got the most tremendous crack on the head. I thought I'd been shot. They'd fractured my skull.

Interviewer: What were your feelings as all this was going on?

Michael: Well, initially, of great shock! In the average vicarage, you don't expect to be bashed over the head with a cricket bat! I was in hospital for a week or ten days, but it wasn't only an attack on me – there were other people in the house as well, and I was obviously concerned about them.

Interviewer: So what happened next?

Michael: They cleared out. I heard the front door bang, and so on. I was unconscious for most of the time, and then one of the other people who'd been attacked managed to get to one of the telephones. We had three or four phones in the house, and they'd cut all the wires except one, which they didn't see. Then the police and the ambulance came, and that was it.

Interviewer: One of the things

that struck a lot of people at the time was that you did say you forgave the people who did this. Could you explain that?

Michael: Yes, but I think there are two separate issues. I was concerned not only about myself but about the others. My view was that you cannot forgive people for something they've done to somebody else. You can only forgive for what is done to you. When it's done to other people, I think we should all demand justice and punishment for people who do that. There's a lot of confusion nowadays.

People think you're supposed to forgive, and other people say that's just wet and wimpish. I think it's wet and wimpish if we forgive somebody for something they've done to someone else. The only person who can really forgive is the victim, and that's a very difficult thing to do, but it's a really important idea for Christians.

In the prayer that Jesus taught, the Lord's Prayer, it says, 'Forgive us our sins, as we forgive those that sin against us.' If we can't do that, then it makes a nonsense of it. It's not a question of whether it will help the other person — it may not. What it will do is help to get rid of bitterness, and desire for revenge, and all those sorts of things. People can't demand it of you — it's a very private business. I was very keen that justice should be done for the sake of the others, and hopeful that I would be able to exercise forgiveness for myself.

Interviewer: And how is everybody, ten years on?

Michael: Well, it's all water under the bridge. We don't go around all torn up about it. One of the other people involved has been doing a great deal of counselling with victims and written a book about it. I've spoken about it in public and written one or two articles at different times, but it's history now.

Interviewer: Thank you very much for talking to us.